ADVENT
GOSPEL
REFLECTIONS

BISHOP ROBERT BARRON

WITH REFLECTION QUESTIONS BY
PEGGY PANDALEON

WORD ON FIRE CATHOLIC MINISTRIES

www.WORDONFIRE.org

INTRODUCTION

Friends,

Welcome, as we begin our Advent journey toward Christmas! Advent is the liturgical season of vigilance or, to put it more mundanely, of waiting. During the four weeks prior to Christmas, we light the candles of our Advent wreaths and put ourselves in the spiritual space of the Israelite people who, through many long centuries, waited for the coming of the Messiah ("How long, O Lord?").

Following them, disciples of the risen Jesus have been waiting in their own times. Paul, Augustine, Chrysostom, Agnes, Thomas Aquinas, Clare, Francis, and John Henry Newman have hence all been Advent people. In fact, the entire Bible ends on a note not so much of triumph and completion as longing and expectation: "Come, Lord Jesus."

During this season, let us join the great men and women of our tradition, turning our eyes and hearts upward and praying, "I am waiting, I am waiting. Come, Lord Jesus."

I look forward to joining you on this journey!

Peace,

+ Robert Barron

Bishop Robert Barron

ADVENT

GOSPEL

REFLECTIONS

NOVEMBER 28, 2021

FIRST SUNDAY OF ADVENT

LUKE 21:25–28, 34–36

*J*esus said to his disciples: "There will be signs in the sun, the moon, and the stars, and on earth nations will be in dismay, perplexed by the roaring of the sea and the waves. People will die of fright in anticipation of what is coming upon the world, for the powers of the heavens will be shaken. And then they will see the Son of Man coming in a cloud with power and great glory. But when these signs begin to happen, stand erect and raise your heads because your redemption is at hand.

"Beware that your hearts do not become drowsy from carousing and drunkenness and the anxieties of daily life, and that day catch you by surprise like a trap. For that day will assault everyone who lives on the face of the earth. Be vigilant at all times and pray that you have the strength to escape the tribulations that are imminent and to stand before the Son of Man."

Friends, in today's Gospel, Jesus tells his disciples to be vigilant. Today marks the beginning of Advent, the great liturgical season of vigilance, of waiting and watching.

What practically can we do during this season of vigil keeping? What are some practices that might incarnate for us the Advent spirituality?

I strongly recommend the classically Catholic discipline of Eucharistic Adoration. To spend a half hour or an hour in the presence of the Lord is not to accomplish or achieve very much—it is not really "getting" anywhere—but it is a particularly rich form of spiritual waiting.

As you keep vigil before the Blessed Sacrament, bring to Christ some problem or dilemma that you have been fretting over, and then say: "Lord, I'm waiting for you to solve this, to show me the way out, the way forward. I've been running, planning, worrying, but now I'm going to let you work." Then, throughout Advent, watch attentively for signs.

Also, when you pray before the Eucharist, allow your desire for the things of God to intensify; allow your heart and soul to expand. Pray, "Lord, make me ready to receive the gifts you want to give," or even, "Lord Jesus, surprise me."

REFLECT: In what ways do you plan to be vigilant this Advent season?

MATTHEW 8:5–11

When Jesus entered Capernaum, a centurion approached him and appealed to him, saying, "Lord, my servant is lying at home paralyzed, suffering dreadfully." He said to him, "I will come and cure him." The centurion said in reply, "Lord, I am not worthy to have you enter under my roof; only say the word and my servant will be healed. For I too am a man subject to authority, with soldiers subject to me. And I say to one, 'Go,' and he goes; and to another, 'Come here,' and he comes; and to my slave, 'Do this,' and he does it." When Jesus heard this, he was amazed and said to those following him, "Amen, I say to you, in no one in Israel have I found such faith. I say to you, many will come from the east and the west, and will recline with Abraham, Isaac, and Jacob at the banquet in the Kingdom of heaven."

Friends, in our Gospel today a Roman centurion comes to Jesus and says, "Lord, my servant is lying at home paralyzed, suffering dreadfully. . . . I am not worthy to have you enter under my roof; only say the word and my servant will be healed."

Any objective observer would say, "Well, this is ridiculous! What this man is asking is impossible." He is not only asking that his servant might be cured; he is asking that he be cured at a distance, with simply a word. He's at the limit of what he could possibly know or control or measure. And yet he trusts; he has faith.

Søren Kierkegaard defined faith as "a passion for the impossible." Is God opposed to reason? Absolutely not; God gave us the gift of reason. Does God want us to be unrealistic? No; he wants us to use all of our powers of imagination and analysis. But faith goes beyond reason; it is a passion for what reason can't see.

That centurion had a passion for the impossible. And that's why Jesus says to him, in some of the highest praise you'll find in the Gospel: "In no one in Israel have I found such faith."

REFLECT: Have you ever, as the centurion, gone beyond reason and relied on faith? Reflect on why or why not.

NOVEMBER 30, 2021

TUESDAY OF THE FIRST WEEK OF ADVENT

Feast of Saint Andrew

MATTHEW 4:18–22

*A*s Jesus was walking by the Sea of Galilee, he saw two brothers, Simon who is called Peter, and his brother Andrew, casting a net into the sea; they were fishermen. He said to them, "Come after me, and I will make you fishers of men." At once they left their nets and followed him. He walked along from there and saw two other brothers, James, the son of Zebedee, and his brother John. They were in a boat, with their father Zebedee, mending their nets. He called them, and immediately they left their boat and their father and followed him.

Friends, in today's Gospel, Jesus calls his first disciples. What is it about this scene that is so peaceful and right? Somehow it gets at the very heart of Jesus' life and work, revealing what he is about. He comes into the world as the second person of the Blessed Trinity, a representative from the community that is God—and thus his basic purpose is to draw the world into community around him.

Jesus says to Simon and Andrew, "Come after me, and I will make you fishers of men." This tells us something about how God acts. He is direct and in-your-face; he does the choosing. "Come after me," Jesus says. He is not offering a doctrine, a theology, or a set of beliefs. He is offering himself. It's as if he's saying, "Walk in my path; walk in imitation of me."

Finally, Jesus explains, "I will make you fishers of men." This is one of the best one-liners in Scripture. Notice the first part of the phrase: "I will make you . . ." This is counter to the culture's prevailing view that we're self-made, that we invent and define our own reality. Jesus puts this lie to bed. We learn from him that it's God who acts, and if we give ourselves to his creative power, he will make us into something far better than we ever could.

REFLECT: How has our culture's focus on being self-made or self-sufficient affected your life and your trust in God's providence? Do you let God act first or do you expect him to "make up" for what you cannot accomplish yourself?

DECEMBER 1, 2021

MATTHEW 15:29–37

A t that time, Jesus walked by the Sea of Galilee, went up on the mountain, and sat down there. Great crowds came to him, having with them the lame, the blind, the deformed, the mute, and many others. They placed them at his feet, and he cured them. The crowds were amazed when they saw the mute speaking, the deformed made whole, the lame walking, and the blind able to see, and they glorified the God of Israel.

Jesus summoned his disciples and said, "My heart is moved with pity for the crowd, for they have been with me now for three days and have nothing to eat. I do not want to send them away hungry, for fear they may collapse on the way." The disciples said to him, "Where could we ever get enough bread in this deserted place to satisfy such a crowd?" Jesus said to them, "How many loaves do you have?" "Seven," they replied, "and a few fish." He ordered the crowd to sit down on the ground. Then he took the seven loaves and the fish, gave thanks, broke the loaves, and gave them to the disciples, who in turn gave them to the crowds. They all ate and were satisfied. They picked up the fragments left over—seven baskets full.

Friends, in today's Gospel, Jesus multiplies the loaves and the fishes. There is no better exemplification in the Scriptures of what I have called the loop of grace. God offers, as a sheer grace, the gift of being, but if we try to cling to that gift and make it our own, we lose it.

The constant command of the Bible is this: what you have received as a gift, give as a gift—and you will find the original gift multiplied and enhanced. One realizes this truth when one enters willingly into the loop of grace, giving away that which one is receiving.

The hungry people who gather around Jesus in this scene are symbolic of the hungry human race, starving, from the time of Adam and Eve, for what will satisfy. We have tried to fill up the emptiness with wealth, pleasure, power, honor, the sheer love of domination—but none of it works, precisely because we have all been wired for God and God *is* nothing but love.

REFLECT: How have you responded to the biblical imperative that what you receive as gift, you should give as gift? Where do you find yourself clinging to what you have and not wanting to give it away?

———————————————————————————————

———————————————————————————————

———————————————————————————————

———————————————————————————————

———————————————————————————————

———————————————————————————————

DECEMBER 2, 2021

MATTHEW 7:21, 24–27

*J*esus said to his disciples: "Not everyone who says to me, 'Lord, Lord,' will enter the Kingdom of heaven, but only the one who does the will of my Father in heaven.

"Everyone who listens to these words of mine and acts on them will be like a wise man who built his house on rock. The rain fell, the floods came, and the winds blew and buffeted the house. But it did not collapse; it had been set solidly on rock. And everyone who listens to these words of mine but does not act on them will be like a fool who built his house on sand. The rain fell, the floods came, and the winds blew and buffeted the house. And it collapsed and was completely ruined."

Friends, today's Gospel challenges us to act on the Good News. On what precisely is the whole of your life built? Your heart or soul is the center of you, the place where you are most authentically and deeply yourself. That is your point of contact with God. There you will find the energy that undergirds and informs all the other areas of your life: physical, psychological, emotional, relational, and spiritual. As such, it is the most important and most elusive dimension of who you are.

If you are rooted in God at the level of your heart and soul, then you will be following the intentions and commands of God, and you can withstand anything. But this does not mean that if we follow God's commands, the winds and floods will not come.

In Jesus' parable, both builders—the one who follows the commands of God and the one who doesn't—experience the rain and the floods that symbolize all the trials and temptations and difficulties at the surface of your life. If at the very center of your life you are linked to God, the storms and floods will come, but they will not destroy you.

REFLECT: On what precisely is the whole of your life built?

_____

_____

_____

_____

_____

_____

_____

_____

_____

_____

DECEMBER 3, 2021

MATTHEW 9:27–31

*A*s Jesus passed by, two blind men followed him, crying out, "Son of David, have pity on us!" When he entered the house, the blind men approached him and Jesus said to them, "Do you believe that I can do this?" "Yes, Lord," they said to him. Then he touched their eyes and said, "Let it be done for you according to your faith." And their eyes were opened. Jesus warned them sternly, "See that no one knows about this." But they went out and spread word of him through all that land.

Friends, today in our Gospel two blind men beg Jesus to heal them.

Blindness in the Bible is very often a symbol of *spiritual* blindness: the incapacity to see what truly matters. Focused on the worldly goods of wealth, pleasure, power, and honor, most people don't see how blind they are to the truly important things: giving oneself to the grace of God and living a life of love. If you have not surrendered to the grace of God, you are blind. How wonderful it is, then, that these men in the Gospel can cry out to Jesus in their need.

They are, of course, making a petition for physical healing, but it's much more than that for us. It's asking for that one thing that finally matters: spiritual vision—to know what my life is about, to know the big picture, to know where I'm going. You can have all the wealth, pleasure, honor, and power you want. You can have all the worldly goods you could desire. But if you don't see spiritually, it will do you no good; it will probably destroy you.

REFLECT: When you pray, do you *truly believe*, as the blind men did, that God will answer your prayer?

MATTHEW 9:35–10:1, 5A, 6–8

*J*esus went around to all the towns and villages, teaching in their synagogues, proclaiming the Gospel of the Kingdom, and curing every disease and illness. At the sight of the crowds, his heart was moved with pity for them because they were troubled and abandoned, like sheep without a shepherd. Then he said to his disciples, "The harvest is abundant but the laborers are few; so ask the master of the harvest to send out laborers for his harvest."

Then he summoned his Twelve disciples and gave them authority over unclean spirits to drive them out and to cure every disease and every illness.

Jesus sent out these Twelve after instructing them thus, "Go to the lost sheep of the house of Israel. As you go, make this proclamation: 'The Kingdom of heaven is at hand.' Cure the sick, raise the dead, cleanse lepers, drive out demons. Without cost you have received; without cost you are to give."

Friends, today Jesus instructs us to pray for laborers for the harvest, for disciples to do the work of evangelization. We need to organize our lives around evangelization. Everything we do ought to be related somehow to it. This doesn't mean that we all have to become professional evangelizers. Remember, you can evangelize by the moral quality of your life. But it does mean that nothing in our lives ought to be more important than announcing the victory of Jesus.

We should think of others not as objects to be used, or annoying people in the way of realizing our projects, but rather as those whom we are called to serve. Instead of saying, "Why is this annoying person in my way?" we should ask, "What opportunity for evangelization has presented itself?" Has God put this person in your life precisely for this purpose?

REFLECT: In what ways do you "announce the victory of Jesus," especially to the annoying people in your life?

_____

_____

_____

_____

_____

_____

_____

_____

DECEMBER 5, 2021

LUKE 3:1–6

*I*n the fifteenth year of the reign of Tiberius Caesar, when Pontius Pilate was governor of Judea, and Herod was tetrarch of Galilee, and his brother Philip tetrarch of the region of Ituraea and Trachonitis, and Lysanias was tetrarch of Abilene, during the high priesthood of Annas and Caiaphas, the word of God came to John the son of Zechariah in the desert. John went throughout the whole region of the Jordan, proclaiming a baptism of repentance for the forgiveness of sins, as it is written in the book of the words of the prophet Isaiah:

A voice of one crying out in the desert:
"Prepare the way of the Lord,
make straight his paths.
Every valley shall be filled
and every mountain and hill shall be made low.
The winding roads shall be made straight,
and the rough ways made smooth,
and all flesh shall see the salvation of God."

Friends, in today's Gospel, Luke quotes from the prophet Isaiah:

"Prepare the way of the Lord,
make straight his paths."(Isa. 40:3)

Advent is a great liturgical season of waiting—but not a passive waiting. We yearn, we search, and we reach out for the God who will come to us in human flesh. In short, we prepare the way of the Lord Jesus Christ.

This preparation has a penitential dimension, because it is the season in which we prepare for the coming of a Savior, and we don't need a Savior unless we're deeply convinced there is something to be saved from. When we have become deeply aware of our sin, we know that we can cling to nothing in ourselves, that everything we offer is, to some degree, tainted and impure. We can't show our cultural, professional, and personal accomplishments to God as though they are enough to save us. But the moment we realize that fact, we move into the Advent spirit, desperately craving a Savior.

In the book of Isaiah (Isa. 64:7), we read:

"Yet, O LORD, you are our father;
we are the clay and you are the potter:
we are all the work of your hands."

Today, let us prepare ourselves for the potter to come.

REFLECT: Are you spiritually passive or active this Advent as you wait for the coming of Jesus? How can you become more spiritually active amid the busyness of the season?

_____

_____

_____

_____

LUKE 5:17–26

*O*ne day as Jesus was teaching, Pharisees and teachers of the law, who had come from every village of Galilee and Judea and Jerusalem, were sitting there, and the power of the Lord was with him for healing. And some men brought on a stretcher a man who was paralyzed; they were trying to bring him in and set him in his presence. But not finding a way to bring him in because of the crowd, they went up on the roof and lowered him on the stretcher through the tiles into the middle in front of Jesus. When Jesus saw their faith, he said, "As for you, your sins are forgiven."

Then the scribes and Pharisees began to ask themselves, "Who is this who speaks blasphemies? Who but God alone can forgive sins?" Jesus knew their thoughts and said to them in reply, "What are you thinking in your hearts? Which is easier, to say, 'Your sins are forgiven,' or to say, 'Rise and walk'? But that you may know that the Son of Man has authority on earth to forgive sins"—he said to the one who was paralyzed, "I say to you, rise, pick up your stretcher, and go home."

He stood up immediately before them, picked up what he had been lying on, and went home, glorifying God.

> Then astonishment seized them all and they glorified God, and, struck with awe, they said, "We have seen incredible things today."

Friends, our Gospel for today tells that wonderful story of the healing of the paralytic. People gather by the dozens to hear Jesus, crowding around the doorway of the house. They bring him a paralyzed man, and because there is no way to get him through the door, they climb up on the roof and open a space to lower him down.

Can I suggest a connection between this wonderful narrative and our present evangelical situation? There are an awful lot of Catholics who are paralyzed, unable to move, frozen in regard to Christ and the Church. This might be from doubt, from fear, from anger, from old resentment, from ignorance, or from self-reproach. Some of these reasons might be good; some might be bad.

Your job, as a believer, is to bring others to Christ. How? A word of encouragement, a challenge, an explanation, a word of forgiveness, a note, a phone call. We notice the wonderful urgency of these people as they bring the sick man to Jesus. Do we feel the same urgency within his Mystical Body today?

REFLECT: Think of a fellow Christian who is "paralyzed" in regard to Christ and the Church. This week, commit to doing something to help her/him move a step closer to the Lord.

DECEMBER 7, 2021

MATTHEW 18:12–14

*J*esus said to his disciples: "What is your opinion? If a man has a hundred sheep and one of them goes astray, will he not leave the ninety-nine in the hills and go in search of the stray? And if he finds it, amen, I say to you, he rejoices more over it than over the ninety-nine that did not stray. In just the same way, it is not the will of your heavenly Father that one of these little ones be lost."

Friends, in today's Gospel, Jesus asks: "If a man has a hundred sheep and one of them goes astray, will he not leave the ninety-nine in the hills and go in search of the stray?" Well, of course not! No self-respecting shepherd would ever think of doing that. If you were a shepherd, you'd cut your losses. That sheep is probably dead anyway if it wandered far enough away.

But we are to understand that God is like that foolish shepherd. God's love throws caution to the wind to seek out the lost sheep. We might expect God to be good to those who are good, and kind to those who follow his commandments. Those who don't, who wander away, are simply lost. God might give them a few minutes, but then they're on their own.

No, God is like this kooky shepherd. God loves irrationally, exuberantly risking it all in order to find the one who wandered away. What good news: God does not love according to a strict justice on our terms, but loves in his own extravagant way.

REFLECT: In what ways have you benefited from God's extravagant love?

_____

_____

_____

_____

_____

_____

_____

_____

_____

_____

_____

_____

_____

_____

LUKE 1:26–38

*T*he angel Gabriel was sent from God to a town of Galilee called Nazareth, to a virgin betrothed to a man named Joseph, of the house of David, and the virgin's name was Mary. And coming to her, he said, "Hail, full of grace! The Lord is with you." But she was greatly troubled at what was said and pondered what sort of greeting this might be. Then the angel said to her, "Do not be afraid, Mary, for you have found favor with God. Behold, you will conceive in your womb and bear a son, and you shall name him Jesus. He will be great and will be called Son of the Most High, and the Lord God will give him the throne of David his father, and he will rule over the house of Jacob forever, and of his Kingdom there will be no end." But Mary said to the angel, "How can this be, since I have no relations with a man?" And the angel said to her in reply, "The Holy Spirit will come upon you, and the power of the Most High will overshadow you. Therefore the child to be born will be called holy, the Son of God. And behold, Elizabeth, your relative, has also conceived a son in her old age, and this is the sixth month for her who was called barren; for nothing will be impossible for God." Mary said, "Behold, I am the handmaid of the Lord. May it be done to me according to your word." Then the angel departed from her.

Friends, today's Gospel shows how Mary became the mother of all the members of the Body of Christ.

From the cross, Jesus pronounced this word to St. John: "Behold, your mother." He was giving Mary not only to John, but through John to the whole Church. Mary would be the mother of all the beloved disciples of Jesus up and down the centuries.

Then we recall that, at the Annunciation, the angel declared to the maiden of Nazareth: "The Holy Spirit will come upon you, and the power of the Most High will overshadow you. Therefore the child to be born will be called holy, the Son of God." The two persons required for the Incarnation were, in other words, the Holy Spirit and the Blessed Mother.

Now we can make the connection: in becoming the mother of Christ, Mary, by extension, would become mother of all of those members of Christ's Mystical Body across space and time. Just as the Holy Spirit and the Blessed Mother were required to bring about the Incarnation in history, so those same two agents are required to bring about the birth of Christ in our souls.

REFLECT: Are you in tune with the work of the Holy Spirit and of the Blessed Mother in your relationship with Christ? Reflect on their subtle yet powerful influence in the Mystical Body of Christ.

DECEMBER 9, 2021

MATTHEW 11:11–15

*J*esus said to the crowds: "Amen, I say to you, among those born of women there has been none greater than John the Baptist; yet the least in the Kingdom of heaven is greater than he. From the days of John the Baptist until now, the Kingdom of heaven suffers violence, and the violent are taking it by force. All the prophets and the law prophesied up to the time of John. And if you are willing to accept it, he is Elijah, the one who is to come. Whoever has ears ought to hear."

Friends, in today's Gospel, Jesus says to the crowds, "From the days of John the Baptist until now, the Kingdom of heaven suffers violence, and the violent are taking it by force." The title for Flannery O'Connor's irresistibly powerful second and final novel, *The Violent Bear It Away*, is taken from the Douay-Rheims translation of this last phrase.

This famously ambiguous passage has given rise to a variety of interpretations over the centuries. Many have taken it to mean that the kingdom of God is attacked by violent people (such as those who killed John the Baptist) and that they threaten to take it away. But others have interpreted it in the opposite direction, as a word of praise to the spiritually violent who manage to get into the kingdom. Flannery O'Connor herself sides with this latter group.

The "violent," on this reading, are those spiritually heroic types who resist the promptings and tendencies of our fallen nature and seek to discipline it in various ways in order to enter into the kingdom of God.

REFLECT: Flannery O'Connor proposes that the violence Jesus speaks of in this passage is positive. Reflect on what it would look like in your own life to become "spiritually heroic."

_____

_____

_____

_____

_____

_____

_____

_____

_____

_____

_____

_____

DECEMBER 10, 2021

FRIDAY OF THE SECOND WEEK OF ADVENT

MATTHEW 11:16–19

*J*esus said to the crowds: "To what shall I compare this generation? It is like children who sit in marketplaces and call to one another, 'We played the flute for you, but you did not dance, we sang a dirge but you did not mourn.' For John came neither eating nor drinking, and they said, 'He is possessed by a demon.' The Son of Man came eating and drinking and they said, 'Look, he is a glutton and a drunkard, a friend of tax collectors and sinners.' But wisdom is vindicated by her works."

Friends, in today's Gospel, Jesus says, "The Son of Man came eating and drinking and they said, 'Look, he is a glutton and a drunkard, a friend of tax collectors and sinners.'"

The Passover meal was decisively important in salvation history. God commands that his people share a meal to remember their liberation from slavery. This supper provides the context for the deepest theologizing of the Israelite community. Both the bitterness of their slavery and the sweetness of their liberation are acted out in this sacred meal.

Jesus' life and ministry can be interpreted in light of this symbol. From the very beginning, Jesus was laid in a manger, for he would be food for a hungry world. Much of Jesus' public outreach centered on sacred meals, where everyone was invited: rich and poor, saints and sinners, the sick and the outcast. They thought John the Baptist was a weird ascetic, but they called Jesus a glutton and a winebibber. He embodies Yahweh's desire to eat a convivial meal with his people.

And of course, the life and teaching of Jesus comes to a sort of climax at the meal that we call the Last Supper. The Eucharist is what we do in the in-between times, between the death of the Lord and his coming in glory. It is the meal that even now anticipates the perfect meal of fellowship with God.

REFLECT: This passage is about the crowd's continuing and contradictory accusations. How does Jesus' concluding statement that "wisdom is vindicated by her works" take the sting out of *any* accusation?

_____

_____

_____

_____

_____

_____

_____

MATTHEW 17:9a, 10–13

*A*s they were coming down from the mountain, the disciples asked Jesus, "Why do the scribes say that Elijah must come first?" He said in reply, "Elijah will indeed come and restore all things; but I tell you that Elijah has already come, and they did not recognize him but did to him whatever they pleased. So also will the Son of Man suffer at their hands." Then the disciples understood that he was speaking to them of John the Baptist.

Friends, today's Gospel passage identifies the appearance of John the Baptist with the expected return of the prophet Elijah. John, the herald of Christ, appears in the desert. Here he stands for all of us in the desert of sin, the lifeless place. It is as though John purposely went there to remind us of our need for grace.

What is he proclaiming? A baptism of repentance. This is the great message. Turn your life over to a higher power. People are coming to him from all sides, because in our heart of hearts we all resonate with this message.

So often in the Old Testament the prophets are asked to act out some quality of the people, perhaps something they were unable or unwilling to see. Well, this tradition continues here: John acts out for the people their helplessness and neediness before the Lord. But then, like Isaiah, he refuses to leave it at that. He announces that one is coming, one who will baptize in the Holy Spirit.

REFLECT: What does it mean to you to "turn your life over to a higher power"? Have you done that completely? What are you holding back?

LUKE 3:10–18

The crowds asked John the Baptist, "What should we do?" He said to them in reply, "Whoever has two cloaks should share with the person who has none. And whoever has food should do likewise." Even tax collectors came to be baptized and they said to him, "Teacher, what should we do?" He answered them, "Stop collecting more than what is prescribed." Soldiers also asked him, "And what is it that we should do?" He told them, "Do not practice extortion, do not falsely accuse anyone, and be satisfied with your wages."

Now the people were filled with expectation, and all were asking in their hearts whether John might be the Christ. John answered them all, saying, "I am baptizing you with water, but one mightier than I is coming. I am not worthy to loosen the thongs of his sandals. He will baptize you with the Holy Spirit and fire. His winnowing fan is in his hand to clear his threshing floor and to gather the wheat into his barn, but the chaff he will burn with unquenchable fire." Exhorting them in many other ways, he preached good news to the people.

Friends, like those in the time of John the Baptist, we ask: "What should we do?" How should we live our lives?

This question, of course, tells us something else about repentance: that it has to do with action more than simply changing our minds. The spiritual life is, finally, a set of behaviors.

So what does John the Baptist tell us to do? His first recommendation is this: "Whoever has two cloaks should share with the person who has none." This is so basic, so elemental—yet so almost thoroughly ignored! In the Church's social teaching, we find a constant reminder that although private property is a social good, the use of our private property must always have a social orientation.

An early Church Father, St. Basil the Great, expressed the idea in tones that echo John the Baptist: "The bread in your cupboard belongs to the hungry. The cloak in your wardrobe belongs to the naked. The shoes you allow to rot belong to the barefoot. The money in your vaults belongs to the destitute. You do injustice to every man whom you could help but do not."

So what should we do this Advent, we who seek repentance, we who await the coming of the Messiah? Serve justice, render to each his due, and give to those who are in need.

REFLECT: How do you use your private property for the common good?

_____

_____

_____

MATTHEW 21:23–27

When Jesus had come into the temple area, the chief priests and the elders of the people approached him as he was teaching and said, "By what authority are you doing these things? And who gave you this authority?" Jesus said to them in reply, "I shall ask you one question, and if you answer it for me, then I shall tell you by what authority I do these things. Where was John's baptism from? Was it of heavenly or of human origin?" They discussed this among themselves and said, "If we say 'Of heavenly origin,' he will say to us, 'Then why did you not believe him?' But if we say, 'Of human origin,' we fear the crowd, for they all regard John as a prophet." So they said to Jesus in reply, "We do not know." He himself said to them, "Neither shall I tell you by what authority I do these things."

Friends, in today's Gospel, the chief priests and elders question Jesus: "By what authority are you doing these things? And who gave you this authority?"

The Greek word used for "authority" is most enlightening: *exousia.* It means, literally, "from the being of." Jesus speaks with the very *exousia* of God, and therefore, his words effect what they say. He says, "Lazarus, come out!" (John 11:43), and the dead man comes out of the tomb. He rebukes the wind and says to the sea, "Be still!" (Mark 4:39), and there is calm. And the night before he dies, he takes bread and says, "This is my body" (Matt. 26:26; Mark 14:22; Luke 22:19). And what he says *is.*

Friends, this is the authority of the Church. If we are simply the guardians of one interesting philosophical perspective among many, then we are powerless. If we rely on our own cleverness in argumentation, then we will fail. Our power comes—and this remains a great mystery—only when we speak with the authority of Jesus Christ.

REFLECT: How can we, mere humans, "speak with the authority of Jesus Christ"?

DECEMBER 14, 2021

MATTHEW 21:28–32

*J*esus said to the chief priests and the elders of the people: "What is your opinion? A man had two sons. He came to the first and said, 'Son, go out and work in the vineyard today.' The son said in reply, 'I will not,' but afterwards he changed his mind and went. The man came to the other son and gave the same order. He said in reply, 'Yes, sir,' but did not go. Which of the two did his father's will?" They answered, "The first." Jesus said to them, "Amen, I say to you, tax collectors and prostitutes are entering the Kingdom of God before you. When John came to you in the way of righteousness, you did not believe him; but tax collectors and prostitutes did. Yet even when you saw that, you did not later change your minds and believe him."

Friends, today's Gospel is the parable of the two sons, a story about obedience to God. To live the good life is not finally a matter of autonomy but of obeying commandments.

The obedience that Jesus desires is a surrender to the one who wants what is best for the surrenderer. The entire to-be of the Son is a listening to the command of the Father, and the creature, consequently, is meant to be nothing but a listening to the command of the Son.

This is why Jesus says in the Gospel of John, "You are my friends if you do what I command you. I do not call you servants any longer. . . . I have called you friends" (John 15:14–15). What was lost in the Garden of Eden was friendship with God, symbolized by the easy fellowship enjoyed by Adam and Yahweh.

The whole of the biblical revelation—culminating in Jesus—could be construed as the story of God's attempt to restore friendship with the human race. In the Last Supper discourse we hear the conditions for this restoration: coinherence with God.

REFLECT: Is there any limit in this life to our opportunity to repent and be forgiven by God? How does repentance facilitate coinherence, or unity, with God?

DECEMBER 15, 2021

WEDNESDAY OF THE THIRD WEEK OF ADVENT

LUKE 7:18b–23

At that time, John summoned two of his disciples and sent them to the Lord to ask, "Are you the one who is to come, or should we look for another?" When the men came to the Lord, they said, "John the Baptist has sent us to you to ask, 'Are you the one who is to come, or should we look for another?'" At that time Jesus cured many of their diseases, sufferings, and evil spirits; he also granted sight to many who were blind. And Jesus said to them in reply, "Go and tell John what you have seen and heard: the blind regain their sight, the lame walk, lepers are cleansed, the deaf hear, the dead are raised, the poor have the good news proclaimed to them. And blessed is the one who takes no offense at me."

Friends, in today's Gospel, John the Baptist summons two of his disciples to ask if Jesus is "the one . . . or are we to look for another?" When this inquiry is conveyed to Jesus, the Lord does not respond theoretically, but rather by pointing to things that are happening. "Go and tell John what you have seen and heard: the blind regain their sight, the lame walk, lepers are cleansed, the deaf hear, the dead are raised, the poor have good news proclaimed to them."

Was Jesus doing all of this in the literal sense? Yes! That he was a miracle worker and a healer was one of the most fundamental perceptions regarding Jesus. When God came among us in Christ, he effected the work of repairing his broken and hurting creation. He is not interested simply in souls but in bodies as well.

And so we hear indeed of the man born blind, of Bartimaeus, of the paralyzed man lowered down through the roof to Jesus, of the woman with the flow of blood, of the man who is deaf and dumb to whom Jesus says "*Ephphatha!*" (Be opened!) (Mark 7:34). We hear of Lazarus and the daughter of Jairus and the son of the widow of Naim.

REFLECT: How are good works an integral part of claiming to believe in Jesus Christ?

_____

_____

_____

_____

_____

_____

_____

_____

_____

LUKE 7:24–30

When the messengers of John the Baptist had left, Jesus began to speak to the crowds about John. "What did you go out to the desert to see a reed swayed by the wind? Then what did you go out to see? Someone dressed in fine garments? Those who dress luxuriously and live sumptuouslyare found in royal palaces. Then what did you go out to see? A prophet? Yes, I tell you, and more than a prophet. This is the one about whom Scripture says:

Behold, I am sending my messenger ahead of you,
he will prepare your way before you.

I tell you,among those born of women, no one is greater than John; yet the least in the Kingdom of God is greater than he."(All the people who listened, including the tax collectors, who were baptized with the baptism of John, acknowledged the righteousness of God; but the Pharisees and scholars of the law, who were not baptized by him, rejected the plan of God for themselves.)

Friends, in today's Gospel, once again the fiery and frightening character of John the Baptist bursts on the scene as the forerunner of Jesus. The opening line is important. Jesus asks the crowds, "What did you go out to the desert to see?" The desert is a place of simplicity and poverty, a place where illusions die, where reality is faced honestly and without compromise.

The Bible frequently employs the desert as the setting for the discovery of bold and simple truths. Advent is, for us, a desert time. It brings us back to the basics.

Now, what does John say in the desert? "Repent, for the kingdom of heaven is at hand" (Matt. 3:2). That wonderful word, "repent," implies a change of mind and vision. John is telling his audience (and us) to wake up and be ready to see something. What does he want us to see? The kingdom, the new order, God's way of doing things. There is a cleaning and a scouring, a rearranging and a renovation that is going to happen. And we have to be ready for it.

REFLECT: What gets in the way of your own vision of the kingdom of God? How can you improve your vision as Advent draws to a close?

_____

_____

_____

_____

_____

_____

_____

_____

MATTHEW 1:1–17

*T*he book of the genealogy of Jesus Christ,
the son of David, the son of Abraham.

Abraham became the father of Isaac,
Isaac the father of Jacob,
Jacob the father of Judah and his brothers.
Judah became the father of Perez and Zerah,
whose mother was Tamar.
Perez became the father of Hezron,
Hezron the father of Ram,
Ram the father of Amminadab.
Amminadab became the father of Nahshon,
Nahshon the father of Salmon,
Salmon the father of Boaz,
whose mother was Rahab.
Boaz became the father of Obed,
whose mother was Ruth.
Obed became the father of Jesse,
Jesse the father of David the king.

David became the father of Solomon,
whose mother had been the wife of Uriah.
Solomon became the father of Rehoboam,

Rehoboam the father of Abijah,
Abijah the father of Asaph.
Asaph became the father of Jehoshaphat,
Jehoshaphat the father of Joram,
Joram the father of Uzziah.
Uzziah became the father of Jotham,
Jotham the father of Ahaz,
Ahaz the father of Hezekiah.
Hezekiah became the father of Manasseh,
Manasseh the father of Amos,
Amos the father of Josiah.
Josiah became the father of Jechoniah and his brothers
at the time of the Babylonian exile.

After the Babylonian exile,
Jechoniah became the father of Shealtiel,
Shealtiel the father of Zerubbabel,
Zerubbabel the father of Abiud.
Abiud became the father of Eliakim,
Eliakim the father of Azor,
Azor the father of Zadok.
Zadok became the father of Achim,
Achim the father of Eliud,
Eliud the father of Eleazar.
Eleazar became the father of Matthan,
Matthan the father of Jacob,
Jacob the father of Joseph, the husband of Mary.
Of her was born Jesus who is called the Christ.

Thus the total number of generations
from Abraham to David
is fourteen generations;
from David to the Babylonian exile, fourteen generations;
from the Babylonian exile to the Christ,
fourteen generations.

Friends, today we read the opening lines of Matthew's Gospel—the first words that one reads in the New Testament. They are a listing of the genealogy of Jesus, the forty-two generations that stretch from Abraham to Christ. If the Word truly dwelt among us, then he was part of a family that, like most, was fairly dysfunctional—a mix of the good and bad. And this is such good news for us.

Let me highlight just two figures from Jesus' family. First, Ruth, who was not an Israelite but rather a Moabite, a foreigner. Some of you reading this feel like outsiders, not part of the "in" crowd, looked at askance by others. Well, the Messiah came forth from Ruth the foreigner and was pleased to be her relative.

Then there is Rahab, a prostitute living and working in Jericho. Are there people reading these words who feel like Rahab? Who think that their whole lives have been sunk in sin? Well, the Messiah came forth from Rahab the prostitute, and he was pleased to be her relative.

The good news of Christmas is that God himself pushed into the dysfunctional and ambiguous family of man.

REFLECT: Think about your own family's "dysfunctions and ambiguities." Where have you seen God work through these issues? How does the ancestry of Jesus give you hope for your own family?

DECEMBER 18, 2021

MATTHEW 1:18-25

*T*his is how the birth of Jesus Christ came about. When his mother Mary was betrothed to Joseph, but before they lived together, she was found with child through the Holy Spirit. Joseph her husband, since he was a righteous man, yet unwilling to expose her to shame, decided to divorce her quietly. Such was his intention when, behold, the angel of the Lord appeared to him in a dream and said, "Joseph, son of David, do not be afraid to take Mary your wife into your home. For it is through the Holy Spirit that this child has been conceived in her. She will bear a son and you are to name him Jesus, because he will save his people from their sins." All this took place to fulfill what the Lord had said through the prophet:

> *Behold, the virgin shall be with child and bear a son,*
> *and they shall name him Emmanuel,*

which means "God is with us." When Joseph awoke, he did as the angel of the Lord had commanded him and took his wife into his home. He had no relations with her until she bore a son, and he named him Jesus.

Friends, in today's Gospel, an angel tells Joseph in a dream to name his son Jesus "because he will save his people from their sins."

The rightful King has returned to reclaim what is his and to let the prisoners go free. The God announced by all the prophets and patriarchs—by Abraham, Jeremiah, Ezekiel, Amos, and Isaiah—is a God of justice, and this means that he burns to set things right. God hates the sin and violence and injustice that have rendered gloomy his beautiful world, and therefore he comes into that world as a warrior, ready to fight. But he arrives (and here is the delicious irony of Christmas) stealthily, clandestinely—sneaking, as it were, unnoticed behind enemy lines.

The King comes as a helpless infant, born of insignificant parents in a small town of a distant outpost of the Roman Empire. He will conquer through the finally irresistible power of love, the same power with which he made the universe.

REFLECT: In what ways can you "conquer through the irresistible power of love" in the battles of your life?

LUKE 1:39–45

*M*ary set out and traveled to the hill country in haste to a town of Judah, where she entered the house of Zechariah and greeted Elizabeth. When Elizabeth heard Mary's greeting, the infant leaped in her womb, and Elizabeth, filled with the Holy Spirit, cried out in a loud voice and said, "Blessed are you among women, and blessed is the fruit of your womb. And how does this happen to me, that the mother of my Lord should come to me? For at the moment the sound of your greeting reached my ears, the infant in my womb leaped for joy. Blessed are you who believed that what was spoken to you by the Lord would be fulfilled."

Friends, today's Gospel tells the marvelous story of the Visitation. At the Annunciation, the angel had told Mary that the child to be conceived in her would be the new David. With that magnificent prophecy still ringing in her ears, Mary set out to visit her cousin Elizabeth, who was married to Zechariah, a temple priest.

No first-century Jew would have missed the significance of their residence being in "the hill country" of Judah. That was precisely where David found the ark, the bearer of God's presence. To that same hill country now comes Mary, the definitive and final Ark of the Covenant.

Elizabeth is the first to proclaim the fullness of the Gospel: "How does it happen to me that the mother of my Lord should come to me?"—the Lord, which is to say, the God of Israel. Mary brings God into the world, thus making it, at least in principle, a temple.

And then Elizabeth announces that, at the sound of Mary's greeting, "the infant in my womb leaped for joy." This is the unborn John the Baptist doing his version of David's dance before the ark of the covenant, his great act of worship of the King.

REFLECT: Without the Holy Spirit, this exchange between Mary and Elizabeth would not have been possible. Reflect on the power of the Holy Spirit in your own life and in the Church.

LUKE 1:26–38

*I*n the sixth month, the angel Gabriel was sent
from God to a town of Galilee called Nazareth,
to a virgin betrothed to a man named Joseph, of the
house of David, and the virgin's name was Mary. And
coming to her, he said, "Hail, full of grace! The Lord
is with you." But she was greatly troubled at what was
said and pondered what sort of greeting this might be.
Then the angel said to her, "Do not be afraid, Mary,
for you have found favor with God. Behold, you will
conceive in your womb and bear a son, and you shall
name him Jesus. He will be great and will be called Son
of the Most High, and the Lord God will give him the
throne of David his father, and he will rule over the
house of Jacob forever, and of his Kingdom there will
be no end."

But Mary said to the angel, "How can this be, since
I have no relations with a man?" And the angel said
to her in reply, "The Holy Spirit will come upon you,
and the power of the Most High will overshadow you.
Therefore the child to be born will be called holy, the
Son of God. And behold, Elizabeth, your relative, has
also conceived a son in her old age, and this is the sixth

month for her who was called barren; for nothing will be impossible for God."

Mary said, "Behold, I am the handmaid of the Lord. May it be done to me according to your word." Then the angel departed from her.

Friends, today's Gospel declares the significance of Mary's *fiat*. When Mary says, "Behold, I am the handmaid of the Lord. May it be done to me according to your word," she exhibits such faith and thereby undoes the refusal of Eve. And this *fiat* to the impossible made possible the Incarnation of God. In accepting the seduction of the alluring Mystery, she allowed God's love to become enfleshed for the transformation of the world.

In the Catholic faith, Mary is praised as the Mother of the Church, the matrix of all discipleship. What this means is that her *fiat* is the ground and model of every disciple's response to God's desire for incarnation. Meister Eckhart said that all believers become "mothers of Christ," bearers of the incarnate Word, in the measure that they acquiesce to the divine passion to push concretely into creation.

REFLECT: In what ways have you said "yes" to the mystery of God? What is the result?

LUKE 1:39–45

*M*ary set out in those days and traveled to the hill country in haste to a town of Judah, where she entered the house of Zechariah and greeted Elizabeth. When Elizabeth heard Mary's greeting, the infant leaped in her womb, and Elizabeth, filled with the Holy Spirit, cried out in a loud voice and said, "Most blessed are you among women, and blessed is the fruit of your womb. And how does this happen to me, that the mother of my Lord should come to me? For at the moment the sound of your greeting reached my ears, the infant in my womb leaped for joy. Blessed are you who believed that what was spoken to you by the Lord would be fulfilled."

Friends, today's Gospel again tells of Mary's visit to Elizabeth. I've always been fascinated by Mary's "haste" in this story of the Visitation. Upon hearing the message of Gabriel concerning her own pregnancy and that of her cousin, Mary proceeded "in haste" into the hill country of Judah to see Elizabeth.

Why did she go with such speed and purpose? Because she had found her mission, her role in the theo-drama. We are dominated today by the ego-drama in all of its ramifications and implications.

The ego-drama is the play that I'm writing, I'm producing, I'm directing, and I'm starring in. We see this absolutely everywhere in our culture. Freedom of choice reigns supreme; I become the person that I choose to be.

The theo-drama is the great story being told by God, the great play being directed by God. What makes life thrilling is to discover your role in it. This is precisely what has happened to Mary. She has found her role—indeed a climactic role—in the theo-drama, and she wants to conspire with Elizabeth, who has also discovered her role in the same drama. And, like Mary, we have to find our place in God's story.

REFLECT: How is your place in God's story related to your vocation as a religious, married, or single person? How is God working through you by means of your vocation?

LUKE 1:46–56

*M*ary said:

"My soul proclaims the greatness of the Lord;
my spirit rejoices in God my savior.
for he has looked upon his lowly servant.
From this day all generations will call me blessed:
the Almighty has done great things for me,
and holy is his Name.
He has mercy on those who fear him
in every generation.
He has shown the strength of his arm,
and has scattered the proud in their conceit.
He has cast down the mighty from their thrones
and has lifted up the lowly.
He has filled the hungry with good things,
and the rich he has sent away empty.
He has come to the help of his servant Israel
for he remembered his promise of mercy,
the promise he made to our fathers,
to Abraham and his children for ever."

Mary remained with Elizabeth about three months
and then returned to her home.

Friends, in today's Gospel, we hear the Magnificat—Mary's great hymn of praise to Yahweh.

The hymn commences with the simple declaration, "My soul proclaims the greatness of the Lord." Mary announces here that her whole being is ordered to the glorification of God. Her ego wants nothing for itself; it wants only to be an occasion for giving honor to God. But since God needs nothing, whatever glory Mary gives to him returns to her benefit, so that she is magnified in the very act of magnifying him. In giving herself away fully to God, Mary becomes a superabundant source of life; indeed, she becomes pregnant with God.

This odd and wonderful rhythm of magnifying and being magnified is the key to understanding everything about Mary, from her divine motherhood, to her Assumption and Immaculate Conception, to her mission in the life of the Church.

REFLECT: Bishop Barron describes Mary in this way: "Her ego wants nothing for itself; it wants only to be an occasion for giving honor to God." Reflect on this fundamental model of discipleship.

_____

_____

_____

_____

_____

_____

DECEMBER 23, 2021

THURSDAY OF THE FOURTH WEEK OF ADVENT

LUKE 1:57–66

When the time arrived for Elizabeth to have her child she gave birth to a son. Her neighbors and relatives heard that the Lord had shown his great mercy toward her, and they rejoiced with her. When they came on the eighth day to circumcise the child, they were going to call him Zechariah after his father, but his mother said in reply, "No. He will be called John." But they answered her, "There is no one among your relatives who has this name." So they made signs, asking his father what he wished him to be called. He asked for a tablet and wrote, "John is his name,"and all were amazed. Immediately his mouth was opened, his tongue freed, and he spoke blessing God. Then fear came upon all their neighbors, and all these matters were discussed throughout the hill country of Judea. All who heard these things took them to heart, saying, "What, then, will this child be?" For surely the hand of the Lord was with him.

Friends, today's Gospel tells the story of the birth and naming of John the Baptist. John's father Zechariah had been rendered speechless after his vision in the sanctuary, but we hear that "his mouth was opened, his tongue freed, and he spoke blessing God."

What follows this passage is the wonderful Canticle of Zechariah, which puts Jesus and John in the context of the great story of Israel.

Once we grasp that Jesus was no ordinary teacher and healer, but Yahweh moving among his people, we can begin to understand his words and actions more clearly. If we survey the texts of the Old Testament—and the first Christians relentlessly read Jesus in light of these writings—we see that Yahweh was expected to do four great things: he would gather the scattered tribes of Israel; he would cleanse the holy temple in Jerusalem; he would definitively deal with the enemies of the nation; and finally, he would reign as Lord of the world.

The eschatological hope expressed especially in the prophets and the Psalms was that through these actions, Yahweh would purify Israel, and through the purified Israel bring salvation to all. What startled the first followers of Jesus is that he accomplished these four tasks, but in the most unexpected way.

REFLECT: The first words Zechariah spoke after being mute for more than six months were in praise of God. How often do you praise God aloud and in the presence of other people?

_____

_____

_____

_____

_____

_____

DECEMBER 24, 2021

FRIDAY OF THE FOURTH WEEK OF ADVENT

LUKE 1:67–79

Z echariah his father, filled with the Holy Spirit,
prophesied, saying:

"Blessed be the Lord, the God of Israel;
for he has come to his people and set them free.
He has raised up for us a mighty Savior,
born of the house of his servant David.
Through his prophets he promised of old
that he would save us from our enemies,
from the hands of all who hate us.
He promised to show mercy to our fathers
and to remember his holy covenant.
This was the oath he swore to our father Abraham:
to set us free from the hand of our enemies,
free to worship him without fear,
holy and righteous in his sight
all the days of our life.
You, my child, shall be called the prophet of
    the Most High,
for you will go before the Lord to prepare his way,
to give his people knowledge of salvation
by the forgiveness of their sins.
In the tender compassion of our God
the dawn from on high shall break upon us,

> to shine on those who dwell in darkness and
>   the shadow of death,
> and to guide our feet into the way of peace."

Friends, in today's Gospel, the Canticle of Zechariah declares how Jesus fulfills the Old Testament's expectations of salvation. I would like to explore two lines of that great prayer today.

The God of Israel, Zechariah prays, "has come to his people and set them free." This is what God always wants to do. He hates the fact that we've become enslaved by sin and fear, and accordingly, he wants to liberate us. The central event of the Old Testament is an event of liberation from slavery. We are, as sinners, enslaved to our pride, our envy, our anger, our appetites, our greed, our lust—all of which wrap us up and keep us from being the people that we want to be.

Zechariah continues: "He has raised up for us a mighty Savior, born of the house of his servant David." God will effect this liberation through the instrumentation of a mighty Savior. This should be read against the background of Israel's long history of military struggle against its enemies. A great warrior has come, and he is from the house of Israel's greatest soldier, David. God had promised that he would put a descendant of David on the throne of Israel for all eternity, and Zechariah is prophesying that this will take place.

REFLECT: How does your faith guard you against fear or liberate you?

DECEMBER 25, 2021

JOHN 1:1–5, 9–14 [OR JOHN 1:1–18]

*I*n the beginning was the Word,
and the Word was with God,
and the Word was God.
He was in the beginning with God.
All things came to be through him,
and without him nothing came to be.
What came to be through him was life,
and this life was the light of the human race;
the light shines in the darkness,
and the darkness has not overcome it.
The true light, which enlightens everyone,
was coming into the world.
He was in the world,
and the world came to be through him,
but the world did not know him.
He came to what was his own,
but his own people did not accept him.

But to those who did accept him
he gave power to become children of God,
to those who believe in his name,
who were born not by natural generation
nor by human choice nor by a man's decision
but of God.

> And the Word became flesh
> and made his dwelling among us,
> and we saw his glory,
> the glory as of the Father's only Son,
> full of grace and truth.

Friends, our Gospel for Christmas day is the prologue to the Gospel of John. In many ways, it is the entire Gospel, indeed the entire Bible, in miniature.

Let's turn to the central passage: "And the Word became flesh and made his dwelling among us." The word used in Greek here for "dwelt" is *eskenosen*, which means literally, "pitched his tent among us." Don't read that in a folksy way. It is meant to call to mind the tabernacle of the temple.

The Word becoming flesh is God coming to dwell definitively in his world, undoing the effects of sin, and turning it into what it was always meant to be. Notice, too, what we see in the wake of this tabernacling: "And we saw his glory, the glory as of the Father's only Son, full of grace and truth."

So John is telling us that Jesus is the new Eden, the new temple, the restored creation, the realization of God's intention for the world. And our purpose is not simply to gaze on this fact with wonder, but rather to enter into its power: "From his fullness we have all received, grace in place of grace."

REFLECT: Faith in Jesus Christ gives us the "power to become children of God," and also to participate in the power of Jesus. How are you using this power? How will you use it more effectively in the future?

CONCLUSION

Friends,

I'd like to thank you for journeying with me through the Advent season. Now that we've finished, you might be wondering, what's next? How do I maintain the spiritual momentum I developed this Advent? I'd like to suggest a few practical tips.

First, be sure to visit our website, WordOnFire.org, on a regular basis. There you'll find lots of helpful resources, including new articles, videos, blog posts, podcasts, and homilies, all designed to help strengthen your faith and evangelize the culture. The best part is that all of it is free!

In addition to those free resources, I invite you to join the Word on Fire Institute. This is an online hub of deep spiritual and intellectual formation, where you'll journey through courses taught by me and other Fellows. Our goal is to build an army of evangelists, people who have been transformed by Christ and want to bring his light to the world. Learn more and sign up at https://wordonfire. institute.

Finally, the best way to carry on your Advent progress is to commit to at least one new spiritual practice. For instance, you might read through one of the Gospels, one chapter per day; or start praying part of the Liturgy of the Hours; or spend some time with the Blessed Sacrament once a week; or decide to attend one extra Mass each week; or pray one Rosary each day, maybe in your car or while you exercise. All of these are simple, straightforward ways to deepen your spiritual life.

Again, thank you from all of us at Word on Fire, and God bless you during this Christmas season!

Peace,

+ Robert Barron

Bishop Robert Barron